From Pivot to Purpose

God continues to open pathways and opportunities, regardless of the challenges we may face.

Triscia Riding

© Copyright 2025 Triscia Riding. All rights reserved
ISBN Soft cover 9781764101608
ISBN ePub 9781764101615

No portion of this book may be reproduced, stored in a retrieval system or transmitted in any form or by any means—electronic, mechanical, photocopy, recording or otherwise—except for brief quotations in printed reviews or promotion, without prior written permission from the author.
Some names and identifying details of people described in this book have been altered to protect their privacy.

Unless otherwise noted, all Scripture is taken from the New International Version®, (NIV) Copyright ©1973, 1978, 1984, 2011 by Biblica, Inc.® Used by permission. All rights reserved worldwide.
Scripture quotations marked ESV are from The Holy Bible, English Standard Version®, copyright © 2001 by Crossway, a publishing ministry of Good News Publishers. Used by permission. All rights reserved.
Scripture quotations marked AMP are taken from the Amplified® Bible (AMPC), Copyright © 1954, 1958, 1962, 1964, 1965, 1987 by The Lockman Foundation. Used by permission.
Scripture quotations marked HCSB are taken from the Holman Christian Standard Bible (HCSB) Copyright © 1999, 2000, 2002, 2003, 2009 by Holman Bible Publishers, Nashville Tennessee. All rights reserved.
Cover art by Ronaldo Dinguamah. Used with permission.
Cataloguing in Publishing Data
Title: From Pivot to Purpose
Author: Triscia Riding
Subjects: memoir, Christian growth, highland dancing, health and illness, spiritual disciplines.
A copy of this title is held at the National Library of Australia

Contents

Foreword	VII
Introduction	VIII
Pivot 1	XI
Pivot 2	XIII
Pivot 3	XVI
Pivot 4	XX
1. Putting God First	1
2. Miracle at the Hospital	11
3. A Jewellery Shop Business?	19
4. When Medical Conditions Look Ominous	25

5. Dealing with Self-worth Issues When Pivoting	31
6. Failed Friendships	41
7. "You Are Always in the Wars"	49
8. Loving and the Forgiving Heart	55
9. Changing My Mindset	63
10. Humble Yourself Before God	69
11. The Escape Clause	73
12. Who Do You Love More Than Any Other?	79
13. Epilogue	85
Appendix	89
Acknowledgements	97

Honesty, identifying, forgiving, and kindness are all words that have come to mind in the reading of this story. A story of a walk in Grace! An enjoyable read!

Pastor Margaret Niethe (retired, Uniting Church)

Triscia's book invites us into her personal experiences of those pivotal moments in time where change is the only option. Her story is highly relatable and will resonate with anyone who has faced significant challenges (particularly health challenges) or stood at a crossroads. Triscia writes with warmth and sincerity, reminding us that grace is present in every step of the journey. Through honest storytelling and spiritual reflection, she offers encouragement and hope. Her message points to the 'pivot points' in life as being divine invitations to grow, to deepen our trust in God, and to reconnect with our true selves. Triscia's story inspires readers to approach their own journey with renewed faith and confidence.

Cheryl Smith (Counsellor, North Lakes QLD)

If physical limitations have caused you to question your place in God's heart, Triscia understands. When life kept forcing changes in her plans, Triscia began a quest to understand God's bigger picture behind it all.

In *From Pivot to Purpose*, she vulnerably shares her search for answers and the practical steps she took to keep asking, seeking, and knocking. These steps have led Triscia into a closer walk with Jesus, and her desire is for readers to experience the same.

Triscia's story shows that you always belong in God's heart and plan, no matter what life throws your way, and if you're willing to pivot a little to change course, new gifts from God await you.

Linda Watt (author of Abundance in the Bush)

Trish shares her life journey through pain and difficulty, showing that the changes that are forced upon us are actually an opportunity given to us by God to go in a new, God-inspired direction.

Rev. Neil Storey (Uniting Church Minister)

Foreword

From Pivot to Purpose is a deeply personal reflection on finding meaning, value, and identity. Triscia tells her story with authenticity, courage, and a compelling humility that gives her readers a glimpse into the wounds and vulnerabilities that can cause us to see ourselves as less than who we truly are.

Through a deepening relationship with God bolstered by accessible spiritual practices, Triscia invites us to look into her life and glean the nuggets of truths that helped her overcome numerous obstacles and pivot to purpose.

This little book is one person's story, but it speaks into universal themes and stories so that each of us can find our place in God's story, a story of love, acceptance and belonging, gifted to us through the grace of Christ Jesus.

Rev. David Chatelier

Introduction

WHAT DOES PIVOTING MEAN?

As a Highland dancer, it struck a chord with me when my pastor's wife described my life in terms of being able to pivot. I saw how good and faithful God has been in all the unexpected twists and turns in my life. When obstacles—often in the shape of a health challenge—meant I was unable to continue using my gifts and talents, God would open new doors—not always immediately—but at the perfect time and with the perfect new gift or talent. But it meant I had to turn slightly or pivot, and so, for me, pivoting means that when I hit a roadblock, I look to God and ask, "Well, what now?"

In the process of exploring God's purposes in all this pivoting, I saw that not all these roadblocks were life-imposed. Some were self-imposed, and if I wanted to pivot into His good plans, any walls of my building needed to be pulled down, not just pivoted away from.

Has life been throwing you curveballs where you suddenly find yourself going in a direction completely different to where you thought you'd be? Or are you feeling blocked by walls you know you've put around yourself? If that's you, I hope your walls are not too tough. But if they are, please hang in there. God really does care, and He will work a miracle in slowly chipping away at those barriers. He will bring you to a place where you are able to believe and have faith in Him with all your heart, soul and mind. You can only achieve what you are looking for through faith.

God began to show me that my experiences might help others—those also searching to grow closer to Him. And so, here I am, inspired by Him to write! This book is the new pivot He is gifting me for, and I hope what I've learned and shared will help you. God has a good plan for you. Pivot a little, and you never know where the next chapter of your life may lead. If it's anything like mine, it's never going to be boring. God will always have your back and will never leave you to execute your pivots alone.

From pivot to purpose, God is ever moving us onwards and challenging us.

Pivot 1

OFF THE CHAMPIONSHIP PODIUM

Highland Dancing originated as a training method used by the Scottish military to prepare men for battle, with a focus on increasing strength and agility. Adapted over time for competitive dancing, it is still very athletic and can be hard on the body. Dancers jump on the balls of their feet, one at a time, stretching both legs to just below the splits up to sixteen times in a row. They also use intricate foot movements and placements while hopping to the beat of the music, sometimes on the spot and sometimes while moving in patterns. The dances continue for up to two and a half minutes. Choreography and display dances last longer, with much shorter rest periods in between than what happens in competitions and championships.

I was a Highland dancer from age seven, absolutely loved it, and could have danced all day, forgetting everything else. I was a top-three competitor in many championships for ten years. In my late teens to early twenties, I suffered shin splint injuries in both legs. I pushed through the pain, but when it intensified during the Scotland World Championships, I realised it was not within my ability to further my competitive career. I faced a choice—either continue to dance sub-standard or embark on something new.

As this was happening, I gave my heart to God, and through people at church, including my husband-to-be, God provided me with a family, His teachings and His love. He gave me something far greater than I had before.

He also enabled me to continue doing what I loved, although I needed to pivot a little in the way I was doing it. I chose to become a Highland Dancing examiner and adjudicator.

Pivot 2

THE STAGE GETS SMALLER

My teaching career began at the age of sixteen, and I became a qualified examiner at twenty, examining around Queensland for over thirty years. At twenty-one, I qualified as an adjudicator and worked in various locations, including Australia, the United States, Canada, and Scotland. It was an honour to be selected to adjudicate the world championships on behalf of Australia in Scotland in 2009.

I was in my early forties when I noticed health issues, pain being the most significant. Brain fog accompanied by five to ten seconds where I was unable to remember what had happened or to remember accurately, and the headaches and migraines that had bothered me since my teenage years were steadily getting worse. A specialist doctor diagnosed me with severe fibromyalgia.

Because of these health challenges, I felt it wasn't in the dancers' best interests that I continue to adjudicate. After thirty years of judging competitions, I resigned as a worldwide Highland Dancing Adjudicator.

With these doors closed, here I was again, asking God, "Well, what now?"

God was very good and pivoted me around to a new door. Towards the end of my adjudicating career, I had begun teaching dancing at a Catholic School. To broaden my scope, my husband built a studio in our front yard, and as it turned out, God allowed me to have one of the bigger Highland Dancing studios in Queensland. Protocol dictated that I not instigate conversations about God, but I was free to answer them when my students asked a question.

I adored teaching and demonstrating and was very protective of my students, particularly when I took them to displays or competitions—a bit like a mother hen. I was proud of their achievements, particularly those who took longer to reach specific milestones throughout their dancing careers. Even today, I love to hear what they are doing, whether it's related to dancing or life in general.

Pivot 3

Can I have this dance?

After marrying, I taught Highland Dancing wherever my husband's work took us. Headaches and neck and back pain hovered in the background, but I was passionate about teaching and demonstrating, and pain relief and prescribed meds enabled me to keep working.

I enjoyed the challenges and opportunities to teach at Australian workshops and dancing camps and was invited to teach in America while there adjudicating. Seeing the difference I could make, encouraging children to be their best and helping them achieve something new or inspire them to rekindle a love of dance, brought me great joy.

The sparkle in their eyes and a smile, even while they were exhausted, gave me a sense of achievement.

My goal wasn't to become the full-time trainer for these students. I wanted them to remain with their original teachers and to help the younger teachers grow and learn alongside their students. Unfortunately, talented dancers were often encouraged to leave inexperienced teachers for more experienced ones. The lack of support for young teachers in training their talented dancers—which would have helped them train future dancers—caused many teachers to leave. This waste of talent was a loss for the Highland Dancing community, so I was passionate about helping develop the skills of young teachers.

Highland Dancing is a dance form that fosters looking for what is wrong with a dancer rather than what is right. The judging system focuses on deducting points instead of awarding them, and the result is many judges and teachers are tuned in to being critical and judgmental.

Attempting to reverse this issue, I wrote a paper to be presented at a worldwide conference on changing methods to embrace a positive rather than negative way of judging. This was another area of passion during my time in Highland Dancing, and while some have agreed with my ideas, many have not. To my knowledge, nothing much has changed as of writing this book.

***

I had always said to God that He would have to hit me over the head pretty hard to stop me from dancing and teaching. Be very careful what you say! In 2009, I stood on a glass coffee table, it broke, and glass sliced through seven ligaments on the top of my right foot, right to the bone. The prognosis of ever dancing again was poor. Doctors weren't even sure I would walk properly again.

A couple of weeks after the accident, a pastor prayed for me. As he did, my toes moved for the first time since my injury. Soon after, I started dancing in my moon boot and went back to dancing and demonstrating almost like it hadn't happened. I delegated a little more and taught without the constant jumping. The pain from my medical conditions remained, but God had given me time to prepare for the changes to come. My thoughts propelled me towards what I would do if I could no longer teach.

I knew it was time to stop when the increased pain medications began affecting my internal organs, and the pain relief wasn't as effective. Setting aside a year to prepare my students and find new teachers, I tried hard to pair the right teacher with the right child. Once I sent my students on, I didn't want them looking back to me for advice instead of their new teachers, so I walked away from Highland Dancing completely.

Some children and parents were sad and didn't understand my decision, but God gave me complete peace, and I knew it was His will and timing. It all happened at the completion of one year, giving the children a fresh start for the next year—a bit like starting a new class at school.

"Well, God, what now?"

Pivot 4

TWISTING AND TURNING

Approaching Christmas 2022, we were short on funds to purchase gifts for the family. I remembered seeing coins set in resin and made into jewellery, and as we had old coins and pre-decimal stamps, my husband bought me a resin kit and I set to work. My early attempts looked very different from the YouTube videos! I persevered, and God was good to me, opening up a new doorway and enabling us to provide gifts for our family when we didn't know how we would.

After much experimentation, trial and error, I discovered a talent for resin work, then added leather plaiting to the mix. Using leather offcuts, I plaited bracelets and then got inspired to try making headbands. I loved wearing headbands, but any I'd worn in the past had given me headaches. *There should be a design that doesn't put pressure on your head!* While thinking and praying about this, God inspired me with a pattern, resulting in a headband that made me feel like I wasn't wearing one at all—no pressure or pain, even after wearing it all day.

As my leather crafting abilities improved and more and more earrings and necklaces were produced, I knew these skills were due to God's grace and gifting. I began to wonder, could this be a small business? A name had been with me since I was a teenager, so I checked online—it was available for use as a business name. Was God prompting me in this direction?

Taking the plunge, I registered 'AquaBlack Design'. My business card logo is made up of the stone that was rolled away from Jesus' tomb, the cross He was nailed to, and the nails. Each nail represents my sins that nailed Him to the cross and held Him there. The stone represents Jesus conquering death and rising from earth to be at God's right hand. It's through all He did that I have the gift of grace. While most of my resin jewellery is generic, some have tiny, handmade wooden crosses embedded and Bible verses or Christian symbols set into the necklaces and bracelets.

I ventured into online marketing and physical markets and set up a workshop in what was my dance studio. To encourage more sales, I entered my leatherwork into the Brisbane Exhibition and was very pleased when I received two third placings: one for round plaiting and one for flat plaiting in the novice section.

And then . . . I fell over my feet and broke a bone in my dominant hand, abruptly stopping the resin and leather work I'd become so passionate about. I was starting to get the idea of this pivoting thing. Waiting with peace in my heart for what was to come next was becoming a little more natural. But there was still a mix of anxiety and impatience as well. "So, what now, God?"

Chapter One

Putting God First

We need to seek and search God out with all our heart and soul if we want to know Him and His will for our lives.

Hand in plaster, I stood talking to my pastor's wife when she made the comment about my life of pivoting. Later, as I meditated on her words, I recognised a pattern in my life—God alters my course, changes my gifts and talents, and pivots me towards something even better. But after this latest incident and asking, "What now, God?" another question surfaced: "What is all this pivoting really about, Lord?"

I wanted to discover His purpose in the way He had led me. "What are you teaching me? What am I really striving towards? What is your goal for me?" As I searched for answers, God handed me a significant challenge. Closed doors weren't always an invitation to pivot. Some doors were shut because I'd built walls in front of them to protect myself from being hurt, and this was affecting my witnessing, self-worth, friendships, diet, health and mindset. I knew I would have to find a way to break down these walls if I was to grow into the person God designed me to become.

When I started journalling answers to "What are you teaching me in all this pivoting, Lord?" an underlying theme bubbled to the surface: I was looking for the approval of others more than His. I was putting people before God. I sensed God saying, "In all of this, you keep looking for people's approval, friendship and acceptance. What about Me? I gave you these gifts and talents. I offer you my friendship. I have forgiven you and loved you more than anyone else ever has or ever could. I loved you so much that I sent my only Son to die for your sins; isn't that enough?"

I began to wonder, *Is this what God is so painstakingly trying to do, to get me to a point where I seek His approval more than people's? Who am I that He would go to so much trouble for me? What will it take to get me on my knees wholeheartedly worshipping God, ignoring others' opinions, and being fully devoted and committed in worshipping and communicating with God to the exclusion of everything and everyone else? How could I reach the place where I was looking for His approval more than people's?*

Yes, I had to admit it. I wanted the acceptance and approval of people far more than I should. I know what it's like to be put on a pedestal when excelling in a sport and receiving trophies on a stage (dancing, in my case), where everyone knows your name, and you don't know theirs. I liked it. I like being on stage, whether leading worship, a Bible study, or teaching people things I have learnt. I like solving problems that other people may be experiencing. I do not enjoy having other people do the same for me nearly as much, nor the experience of accepting help, although the older I get, the more accepting I'm becoming.

My starting point in the face of these challenges was to set a timer for regular prayer and Bible reading. Prioritising this habit became a huge blessing, although seeing the benefits took a few months. I know this may sound like a long time, but I'm very stubborn, so it took a while to get through this very tough exterior!

Secondly, I journalled, and as I did, God brought into focus certain roadblocks, highlighting areas where I had put people before Him. These revelations led to a very intense struggle, but I knew I could only move towards a closer relationship with Him if I dealt with these issues.

One by one, God brought people to mind, and I knew He was challenging me to witness to them, regardless of what they would think of me. The problem was that they had no time for Christians. Some had selflessly invested a lot in my life over the years for no personal gain, and often when I most needed them. I felt I owed it to them to share what God has done for me. I thought if I didn't witness to them, I would have done nothing to prevent them from entering eternity without God. I was to share my faith honestly.

I would need God's armour, strength and courage to share my faith and keep moving forward—no matter how their opinion of me might change. I asked God for wisdom to be able to explain to others clearly what He means to me. As I followed through on this first challenge, I understood it didn't mean I had to be an evangelist spouting religious propaganda, and I didn't have to try to convert them, although I should want to show them God's love.

More than anything, I wanted to be in a relationship with God with no embarrassment on my part when with non-believers, where I can be a Christian, expressing myself openly and freely. Because I struggle with words when speaking face-to-face, I sent these people hand-written letters. My husband and I pray that these letters are not discarded or forgotten and that they may plant seeds that open their eyes to who God is.

My pride slowly started to crumble, but this was just the beginning. Many other stumbling blocks would need removing along the journey. Writing this book has been one of the ways that has helped to change my mindset and to seek God's approval first. Through this, He has opened up areas of my life where I have been failing or struggling and has shown me steps to walk closer with Him. You'll find these steps in the Appendix.

As you read, my hope is you will be strengthened to stand firm and solid in God's loving arms as the confident child God intended you to be, regardless of how others may see, treat, or respond to you. It may not take you as long as it did me to break down your walls. And 'wall' may not be the right word for you, but it describes a barrier to what you want to happen—anything that is preventing you from stepping into freedom, any obstacle that needs to be traversed or removed so you can continue running the race toward God, growing in spiritual maturity, becoming the person God created you to be.

I encourage you to start this journey to freedom by working through Scripture and journalling as you go. God has given us steps to follow in His Word, the Bible. Ask Him to reveal anything He wants to bring to your attention so you can discover His purpose in the way He is leading you and step into the good plans He has for your life.

Let's walk forward towards what God wants to teach us through the pivots in our lives so we can move from pivot to purpose. And let's trust the Holy Spirit to help us demolish any walls blocking our freedom.

Scripture

> Am I now trying to win the approval of human beings, or of God? Or am I trying to please people? If I were still trying to please people, I would not be a servant of Christ.
> Galatians 1:10

> As He was leaving on His journey, a man ran up and knelt before Him and asked Him, "Good Teacher [You who are essentially good and morally perfect], what shall I do to inherit eternal life [that is, eternal salvation in the Messiah's kingdom]?" Jesus said to

him, "Why do you call Me good? No one is [essentially] good [by nature] except God alone. You know the commandments: 'Do not murder, Do not commit adultery, Do not steal, Do not testify falsely, Do not defraud, Honor your father and mother.'" And he replied to Him, "Teacher, I have [carefully] kept all these [commandments] since my youth." Looking at him, Jesus felt a love (high regard, compassion) for him, and He said to him, "You lack one thing: go and sell all your property and give [the money] to the poor, and you will have [abundant] treasure in heaven; and come, follow Me [becoming My disciple, believing and trusting in Me and walking the same path of life that I walk]." But the man was saddened at Jesus' words, and he left grieving, because he owned much property and had many possessions [which he treasured more than his relationship with God] Mark 10:17-22 AMP.

For this man, the 'wall' he wasn't prepared to break down was his riches. Riches will never get us into heaven, and our approval ratings won't keep us company in heaven.

Challenge: For me, people's approval came before God. What is it for you? Let's choose who we want to impress with a long-term plan in mind.

Chapter Two

Miracle at the Hospital

Don't forget to ask God to prepare the way, particularly when you are in pain.

So often, I forget how much God has given me and how much I have to be thankful for every time a pivotal event happens in my life. The pivots I've shared so far are just a snippet from my life to give you an idea of what can crop up and how God is good and faithful in how He deals with us in each situation. So, if I still have your attention, let me tell you more about my story and how God is working with me to help me grow a little more each day.

When I wrote this chapter, I was in hospital. Intense pain in the upper part of my stomach landed me in the Emergency Department of the local hospital and resulted in surgery late that evening. The doctor told me that I was very lucky, as even an hour or two delay and parts of my small bowel may not have recovered. It had adhered, causing a complete obstruction, and part of my bowel would have died.

The whole time I was waiting for treatment, I was praying for the right doctor, nurses, and surgeon, and God delivered. Up until just before surgery, the surgeon wasn't sure what he would find when he went in and whether to wait a little longer or not. The CT scan and ultrasound results didn't make sense to him, so he decided to operate. God was surely there and in control.

It was only through prayer that I was able to feel complete peace that everything was going to be okay when I eventually went into surgery. I left it all in God's hands, not knowing whether they would have to open me up completely or if it would be keyhole surgery. I'm grateful it turned out to be the latter.

The staff were all so nice, and I felt God was really looking after me the whole time I was in hospital. Even the people I was in the ward with were easy to get along with. I should have been stressed, but when I gave it into God's hands, that peace I felt was just what I needed. His loving hands were definitely on me that day.

In Daniel 3:16-28, we read about Meshach, Shadrach and Abednego. These men were told to serve the gods of Nebuchadnezzar and worship the golden image he set up. They would be cast into a fiery furnace if they did not fall down and worship the image. They refused to worship any other god but their God and said that the God whom they serve is able to deliver them from the furnace and out of the hand of the king. But even if He didn't, they wouldn't deny their God.

The king was furious and made the furnace seven times hotter before having the three men bound and thrown into the furnace. The men who were ordered to throw them into the furnace were killed by the exceedingly hot flames. But when Nebuchadnezzar looked into the fire, he saw not three, but four men loose and walking around in the fire, not hurt at all. So he called them out of the fire and saw that not even a hair on their heads was singed, nor the smell of smoke on their clothes.

My medical situation was nothing like Meshach, Shadrach, and Abednego's. Still, in every scary circumstance, we have God's Word to look towards, to remind us that He has rescued people in the past from far more difficult situations than we might find ourselves in.

God is with you and me, just as He was with those men in the fire. Rejoice in His healing, loving hands placed on you as you go through medical procedures or episodes of pain and suffering. Believe in the One who sent His Son to redeem and reconcile us so we could become joint heirs of the one and only God, our Father. In times of stress and worry, remember that our troubles will all eventually pass away once we reach heaven. And always remember to pray in all situations because our troubles will grow strangely dim as we gaze upon Jesus' face.

While I was in hospital, I let my pride and emotions get in the way of sharing my faith and identity as God's child, even though I had a perfect opportunity. I wasn't sure how to begin a faith conversation with the other patients without making it sound contrived or unnatural. That's not the way for people to get a good impression of Christians! I want people to see Christians as normal, nice, caring, intelligent people.

A lady there went from bed to bed, praying for people. *Should I have done the same, praying for those in the beds next to me? Would it have benefited them if I had started trying to pray for them openly?* I don't know, but I didn't even pray for them silently. I was too concerned with what was going on in my own little world.

I felt this was a minor setback in me standing tall as a child of God. As I talked to Him about whether I should have boldly approached people and spoken to them about my faith, I felt He was giving me a "You're doing okay" on this one. Or maybe "You're not ready yet." He is so patient with me. Who else would put up with being put to the back and hidden in embarrassment? And still, He is there to bail me out; He loves me, saves me, heals me, and calls me His child. I let Him down in so many ways, yet day after day, He is there with outstretched arms, waiting for me.

We never know when a seed will sprout, and God calls us to plant a seed wherever we are. We don't always need to be the ones to nurture it and help it grow. Each opportunity should be evaluated individually and prayed about. Some may feel God calling them to witness or pray for the patients beside them. To comfortably share what God has done for us and in our lives, we need to be confident of His leading. Yes, we are called to be witnesses, but let's remember not to stress over trying to do everything.

Scripture

> Do not be anxious about anything, but in every situation, by prayer and petition, with thanksgiving, present your requests to God. And the peace of God, which transcends all understanding, will guard your hearts and your minds in Christ Jesus. Philippians 4:6-7

But you will receive power and ability when the Holy Spirit comes upon you; and you will be My witnesses (to tell people about Me) both in Jerusalem and in all Judea, and Samaria, and even to the ends of the earth. Acts 1:8 AMP

Challenge: Write out your testimony so you will be more prepared to share your faith journey with others. Ask God to give you the opportunities and wisdom to know when and who to share this with.

Chapter Three

A Jewellery Shop Business?

Whether it's the mundane or the dramatic, God wants to be involved in every aspect of our lives.

Four weeks after the cast went on my hand, God was good and gracious to me and healed my hand, and the cast came off. No further medical care was necessary. Although still experiencing pain, I used leather plaiting as a physiotherapy exercise. Each day, my hand regained a little more flexibility and strength. I resumed jewellery making, but was still unsure where God wanted me to go with this.

I hoped to speak with people and reach them through my resin and leather work. *But how would I get my jewellery out to the public and let people know I existed, especially when I was struggling with social media to get my products known?* On a usual Monday morning outing with my mother, we came across a co-op store in a local shopping centre. The lady running this franchise just happened to be there. She seemed to like my jewellery and explained how the co-op worked. I could lease a small bookcase for $230 a week, work four hours a week at the store, and my goods would be on sale in a major shopping centre all week. This appeared to be the perfect platform to sell my jewellery.

I spoke to my husband and left it in God's hands, wondering if this would be another pivot in my life. I knew if it was not to be, God would eventually show me what He had in store for me and my jewellery, and it would be better than I had ever imagined.

It seems there is always another twist and turn in my life. I thought the co-op was the way God wanted me to go when, lo and behold, a friend turned up who was using 'Shopify', an online store where I'd been looking at selling my jewellery. I had found this whole process difficult to navigate. Several hours later, with a checklist of things I needed to do before being able to 'go online,' I wondered whether I should go the online shopping route. When it comes to the material side of things, it can be confusing when we want to do our work for God, but the process we must go through to get there is secular.

Months down the track, with some sales through the co-op and no progress with the online shop, I put a hold on those and enjoyed doing the occasional market when I was invited to attend. I was still unsure where this was all going, but I felt less stressed by the need to succeed.

I've always felt the need to succeed in the world's eyes, but I haven't known what it means to succeed in God's eyes. I'm trying to take things a little slower, wait on God's timing, and be patient, but behind it all, I've felt a little deflated and unsure of God's plan for me. I know He has a plan. He created me uniquely for a purpose, but

I still can't clearly see what that unique purpose is. But I will continue to step forward into any opportunities that come my way that I think may be from God. I will continue to develop the skills and talents God has gifted me with for as long as they are gifted to me. And I will hope and pray that He will use me as a vessel to further His work on earth.

Knowing whether something is from God and how it fits in with His plan is hard. *Is what I'm doing going in the direction He wants, or is this just the direction I want because I can see that this way will make some profit?* Prayer and taking that step forward is the only way I know to work through that question. If we sit still and do nothing, it's a bit like the man caught in a flood, sitting on top of his roof. A boat comes to pick him up, but he says to the driver, "No, I'm waiting for God to rescue me." Then a helicopter hovers over and lowers a rope, but he says, "No, I'm waiting for God to rescue me." He eventually drowns, and in heaven, he asks God, "Why didn't you rescue me?" God says to him, "I sent you a boat and a helicopter. What more did you want?"

We need to take what is in front of us and use it. If it's not to be, it won't happen. Pray for God to bless the opportunities if that's the way He wants you to go or to take them away if it's not. There is always another door just around the corner, another pivot we can make. The more we trust and believe in Him, the more He will continue to bless us abundantly.

Even with all the stepping out in faith, God may say, "I want you to walk away from this. Are you prepared to do that?" And the answer will always need to be "Yes." Because the gift to do any of this in the first place came from God, it belongs to Him. We need to be ready to step out in faith, but also to give it all back to God whenever He asks, because it never belonged to us in the first place.

Scripture

> So I say to you: Ask and it will be given to you; seek and you will find; knock and the door will be opened to you. For everyone who asks receives; the one who seeks finds; and to the one who knocks, the door will be opened.

Which of you fathers, if your son asks for a fish, will give him a snake instead? Or if he asks for an egg, will give him a scorpion? If you then, though you are evil, know how to give good gifts to your children, how much more will your Father in heaven give the Holy Spirit to those who ask him! Luke 11:9-13

Trust in and rely confidently on the LORD with all your heart and do not rely on your own insight or understanding. Proverbs 3:5 AMP

Challenge: It's a struggle to put everything you've worked hard for in the hands of someone else and say, "It's all yours. You can decide whether it goes or stays." But this is what trusting God looks like. What needs to change in you so you can let go of your plans and trust God's agenda for your life?

Chapter Four

When Medical Conditions Look Ominous

Prioritise God first, and then you will be able to handle the hard situations better.

Initial responses to medical issues see us running for answers from professionals or now the internet, but we need to remember that God already knows what is in store and has it all under control. We need to put our health in His hands and trust Him.

'Long-term', 'ongoing', and 'not going to improve' describe many of my medical conditions. I know these aren't as bad as 'terminal'. On my good days, I accept this is my life and just get on with it. I struggle to cope on bad days, especially when everything hurts, and positivity quickly melts away. These days, all I see are the negatives: I'm a drain on resources, a pain to be around, life's not fair, and woe is me.

Medical tests are commonplace for me, and the results I'm waiting on while writing this section of the book are the cause of the thickening in my stomach wall. Doctors say one explanation is cancer. Should it be, I know God has it under control. I've put this in His hands and trust Him to look after whatever is going on. He has already provided so many miracles for me. But mostly, when I look at the work still to be done and the gifts and talents He has given me, I feel quietly confident that my work on earth is not yet over.

God is pleased when we use the gifts He's given us. But those things we create and the projects we have to finish or accomplish for Him are never more important than the One who gives us our gifts and talents. In all our 'doing', it's more important to stop and listen to what He has to say. It's more important to remember to thank Him for all He has done and provided.

I now have the test results and am grateful no cancer was detected. Even if there are more medical obstacles in my path ahead, I know God will be right there with me, and we will work through them together. Whatever lies ahead, nothing can take away the joy and peace He has placed in my heart or the grace He has given me—that free gift of grace. If we allow Him to, God will always give us joy, peace, and an indescribable calmness, no matter how ominous circumstances may appear.

During an endoscopy, five to six biopsies were taken. I knew I'd need to consider a diet, which I wasn't looking forward to (I love my chocolate and lollies, and there may be other foods on the no-go list as well), but I wasn't expecting anything nasty to come back in the results. Even if there was, God had it under control. I put it in His hands and trusted Him to look after whatever was going on.

The Bible says that our bodies are His temple. Unfortunately, I haven't treated this one that way. It may not have been in perfect working order when I got it, but that was no excuse. I still should have put more effort into it while enjoying life. The Bible also says that no food is bad for us but that everything should be taken in moderation. This is where my problems come in, and my struggle with a few food-related issues and cravings gives me grief. Daily asking God to help helps! But sometimes, we need the help of friends or professionals who can support us in our journey towards getting it under control—if it becomes out of control. God knows my struggle, and this is something that cannot be shrugged off quickly or easily.

Further results are finally in, and it's off to surgery, but not until I lose weight, and my way of eating needs to change forever. The results were a total surprise as I was found to have over two hundred acid reflux episodes per day. I needed to have a new valve made from part of my stomach to replace a malfunctioning one. Fast forward a couple of months, and after losing 12 kilograms, I had surgery where they made a new valve leading into my stomach.

They also found a hiatus hernia. I'm learning to eat in a new way and slowly introducing foods, only to discover sugar is no longer my friend, as anything I eat with sugar causes bad headaches. I guess God is helping me look after this body a little better. He's been so good to me in that there was nothing more serious wrong.

The churches of Macedonia were in an ordeal of severe tribulation, but their abundance of joy and their depth of poverty together overflowed in a wealth of lavish generosity (2 Corinthians 8:1-5). Even though you may be living with pain and facing tribulation, you have unique abilities and gifts, and if you look up and turn your head or pivot just a little, God will show you amazingly beautiful gifts just for you and beauty that is just within reach. He will give you joy and peace within your pain, and He will give you purpose. But first, you have to be willing to open the door to let Him in, pivot around to see the door waiting for you, and open it.

Scripture

> May all those who seek You (as life's first priority) rejoice and be glad in You; May those who love Your salvation say continually, "Let God be magnified!" Psalm 70:4 AMP

Challenge: What medical challenges are leading you to a different way of life that may be opening up a new direction for God to use you for His glory and purpose? Look to your left and your right; seek, and you just might find something wonderful He has in store for you.

Chapter Five

Dealing with Self-worth Issues When Pivoting

You were created unique. There is no one else like you in all the world. A loving Father purposefully created you for a unique purpose that you are uniquely qualified to fulfil. You are not a mistake.

Dealing with the disappointment of not being able to do something I loved and then moving on to something new has been difficult. I've had to deal with feelings of being useless because of health limiting what I was physically able to do. Watching people my age doing so much more than I'm able is hard to take some days and can make me feel less than able-bodied. Sitting and watching while my husband did all the work or paying someone else to do it made me feel useless. I'd notice household jobs needing to be done, and despite knowing the intense pain that would follow, I'd often do them, resulting in days of being unable to do anything. I don't learn things the easy way, or, it seems quickly. I felt I was letting my husband down as his wife, a mother and a friend. My medical expenses were high, and my inability to perform basic housework meant getting house cleaners in, contributing to extra expenses. Travel and other outings were no longer possible. Depression wasn't far below the surface most days.

Going from being strong, able-bodied and fending for yourself to relying on someone else is a real eye-opener in humility and a lesson in dealing with self-worth. It's hard in these circumstances to remember that our self-worth doesn't come from what we can do physically. Our closeness to God is far more important to Him and is the source of our spiritual power. Our walk with God will last for eternity; our walk here on earth is but a blink of the eye in comparison. And so I'm learning that we walk in grace, not in works. We have a faith-based relationship with God, not based on what we do but on what we believe.

Lack of self-worth can lead to the inability to believe others love us for who we are and to question, *Do they really like me? Are they doing things for me because they care and are being kind, or because they feel obligated?* This can lead to testing their friendship or love to see if it's real. We can push away the people who do love and care for us, and it becomes a vicious cycle as we tell ourselves, *Well, they mustn't have loved us very much if they couldn't stand by us while we were testing their loyalty and love.* Yet, if we were tested the same way, would we fare any better?

I think the devil loves to tell us we aren't good enough. It may be one of his great little triumphs in this world. But we need to start spreading the truth that he is so very wrong. We are good enough to have friends and loved ones accept us just as we are. And we should love and accept ourselves just as we are because Jesus has.

I've had Christian people who I looked up to and admired let me down or tell me I wasn't worth the effort. But Romans 5:6-11 talks about how while we were still sinners, God accepted and loved us and thought us worthy of sending His only Son to die for us. We are worth the effort to God, so don't believe the lies; only believe the truth you read for yourself in God's Word. And only listen to His Holy Spirit.

It's amazing when God chooses to reveal things to us. I was doing the dishes and having a chat with God about a difficult situation I had to face, and He revealed a truth about my self-worth issues from an early age. I was always trying to measure up to what others wanted me to be, always trying to be what someone else thought I should be, to achieve some goal set for me by somebody else. I never thought I was good enough just to be me. Now I know that I am good enough, that I am exactly who I am meant to be, that God created me to be just the person I am, and that He loves me as I am. I don't have to change into another person or achieve great goals for Him to accept me because He already has accepted me. He has already chosen me just the way I am. Anything else I do is a response I make out of love for what He has done for me. It's not a requirement; it's not a demand or set of instructions that must be met to retain His love and acceptance. Simply a free will expression of love for such an amazing love gifted to me; grace given freely and without asking for anything in return but for me to accept His gift. WOW!!

Finding your self-worth is knowing that God chose you. He sent His Son to die for you. He decided He wanted you in His family, as His child. Now it's up to you to accept that. It's up to you to accept His free gift of grace and the freedom that brings. You don't have to do anything to achieve His love or acceptance. You don't have to jump through any hoops or work through any workbooks and tick off a list of achievements. You just have to believe and trust in Him and you have complete freedom in Him.

It all sounds so simple. The thing is that it is. The problem for most of us is that it's so hard to get our heads around the fact that we don't have to do anything other than believe and accept. We're used to people expecting something in return. *You don't get anything for free, and everyone expects something in return.* We struggle that acceptance by God is not works-based but only faith-based.

So, this is where it gets tough. Feeling great about yourself isn't an instant or permanent fix. There will be ups and downs, but you need to keep coming back to the above and claiming Scripture promises. Try to find a group that will support and accept you for who you are. I've found that this is no easy thing to do, particularly when you don't believe in yourself, but it is well worth the effort.

Breaking down this wall will require reading the Bible over and over to let it sink in. Find commentaries in an easy-to-understand language. What works for me is an online Bible app with free commentaries and others I can purchase as an option. I'll list the app in the Appendix. In all the commentaries and research, God's Word is the one true word. Before you start reading, ask God through His Holy Spirit to provide wisdom and discernment to reveal His truth. Don't forget to put on the Armour of God and ask for God's protection against any deceit from the prince of deceit, Satan (Ephesians 6:10-18, see below). We must remember we are fighting a war on two fronts, physical and spiritual. So, if you want the absolute truth, start out well prepared and don't let yourself be deceived along the way by false teachings.

I'm certainly not an exhaustive encyclopedia. I have a lot to learn myself. Let me know how you go. I'm always open to learning more on this topic.

Scripture

> The Lord your God has chosen you out of all the peoples on the face of the earth to be his people, his treasured possession. Deuteronomy 7:6

> You did not choose me, but I chose you. John 15:16

> Then Moses said to the Lord, "Please, Lord, I am not a man of words (eloquent, fluent), neither before nor since You have spoken to

Your servant; for I am slow of speech and tongue." The Lord said to him, "Who has made man's mouth? Or who makes the mute or the deaf, or the seeing or the blind? Is it not I, the Lord? Now then go, and I, even I, will be with your mouth, and will teach you what you shall say." Exodus 4:10-12 AMP

Moses struggled with feelings that he wasn't good enough, but God kept telling him he was. God came up against every one of Moses' excuses as to why he wouldn't be a good person to use to set His people free from Egyptian slavery.

Finally be strong in the Lord and in the strength of his might. Put on the whole armor of God, that you may be able to stand against the schemes of the devil. For we do not wrestle against flesh and blood, but against the rulers, against the authorities, against the cosmic powers over this present darkness, against the spiritual forces of evil in the heavenly places. Therefore take up the whole armor of God, that you may be able to withstand in the evil day, and having done all, to stand firm. Stand therefore, having fastened on the belt of truth, and having put on the breastplate of righteousness, and, as shoes for your feet, having put on the readiness given by the gospel of peace. In all circumstances take up the shield of faith, with which you can extinguish all the flaming darts of the evil one; and take the helmet of salvation and the sword of the Spirit, which is the word of God, praying at all times in the Spirit, with all prayer and supplication. Ephesians 6:10-18 ESV

Challenge: Try to deepen your understanding of what God says about your value to Him by using a Bible commentary. You could start by studying the scriptures quoted in this chapter.

Chapter Six

Failed Friendships

It is so easy to isolate and keep to ourselves, but we all need friendship and support in our Christian walk.

Friendships can be difficult for people with medical conditions because some illnesses come with embarrassing side effects. One lady I knew was very self-conscious about her coughing. I hardly noticed it, but it kept her from socialising. For me, it can be constant headaches and not explaining that I'm withdrawing because of the pain. I also suffer from irritable bowel syndrome, and the resulting gas problem can be a social killer, as can other side effects.

Over the years, I've had uncomfortable experiences and received hurtful comments (some unintended, some intended). There are times when I've put effort into a friendship only to have it spurned or treated as nothing, again by people who I thought were Christian friends. It's not the case with most genuine Christians who do care about people, but often, it seems people don't really care or want to hear about what is going on in your life. Conversations fall flat unless the focus is on them, their hobbies, or gossip about someone's misfortune or downfall.

I struggle to make conversation others are interested in. There are always the latest TV shows to discuss, but I find little value in small talk and time-wasting conversations. A topic I could really enjoy, really sink my teeth into, would be God, His Son, Jesus Christ, and the Holy Spirit. I'm not good with remembering verses, but these conversations would certainly interest me. Usually, though, people do not want to discuss spiritual matters when they get together socially.

To be fair, I am far from perfect in the ways of friendship and have very few long-standing, solid friendships. I had been withdrawn for a long time and had been hard to get to know, not allowing others into my circle who weren't already there or hadn't tried to get to know me. So, you can see why I failed at friendships. *Maybe I need to go to night school to learn how to do it right!!! Any thoughts or helpful hints here, God?* Have I focused on my troubles so much that I've failed to look at what is happening around me? Have I been too excited telling people all about what has been happening in my life that I haven't heard or seen what was happening in their day, week, family, health, and hobbies? Have I failed just to be silent and listen?

As I thought more about why friendships have not always worked for me, one problem I recognised was seeking friends who fit me. I already have the best fit with Jesus. He listens to me and knows me better than anyone else ever will. But I now need to model that friendship toward others without expecting anything in return, just as Jesus did with me.

My growth in this area started with God showing me I was like a turtle retreating into my little shell and keeping the rest of the world out. My thinking was, *I don't need anyone. I'm quite happy not letting anyone else in; that way, no one can hurt me or disturb my comfortable little setup.* But I also discovered that my heart had forgotten how to melt and how to love. It had become hard and cold, and I knew it was time for it to thaw. It was time to poke my head out of my shell, see what was happening in the world, and chance being hurt again.

The shell had to go! I couldn't just pivot away, so I started excavating this wall by opening my eyes to see who needed prayer, who needed my help, and who may want to be my friend. Learning to love people is the key, whether they become friends or not (and it isn't easy to build friendships if people reply to conversation in single words). We are called to follow in Jesus' footsteps. He loved us—the sinners, the unloved. Just as God loved us before we knew Him, we are called to love others before they really know us, even if they eventually reject us. We can't know others as deeply as Jesus does, but we can listen and respond with agape love.

I've also realised I don't need a hundred friends or to worry about long-term relationships. God has this covered, as He is always by my side and has graciously provided some longtime friends. One friend sticks by me through thick and thin and has always been a phone call away, no matter how long it's been since I've seen her. God blessed me the day we met, and it just so happens she is helping me with this book.

God didn't say we wouldn't get hurt in our journey through life, but He did say He would stand by us. He also didn't make us perfect. For every time we are hurt, there is probably a person we have unknowingly hurt ourselves. We must honestly own up to that to face the hurt we will experience in the real world.

We all need friendship and support in our Christian walk. Ideally, we can find a Christian group to accept us for who we are. This is no easy thing to do, particularly when you are self-conscious about your health and don't want to explain your personal issues to every new person who joins the group.

I imagine those motivated to facilitate this type of sensitive Christian support group are typically not those experiencing the problems. People who need such groups are usually shy and uncomfortable around others already because of embarrassing side effects or low self-worth from a long-term illness.

How do we solve this problem? First, we ask God to help us. It's always a good start! Second, consider that maybe God is asking you (and me) to take a big breath and lead a group ourselves. If this is the case, be clear in your mind what your group will be about and what you want to study. I made the mistake of starting conversations without having my goals written down. Because I have a problem putting things into words when face-to-face with people, when I went to explain what I wanted and what the group was all about, it sounded like gibberish!

Next, talk to your pastors and, with their blessing, approach people one at a time after church. A group, like I'm suggesting, is quite specific, so look for people you are comfortable with. Try to find common interests. Advertise in the newsletter if there is one. And even if you begin with just two people, make a start.

It's important to try to be regular in your meetings; otherwise, people can quickly lose interest and fall away.

Your confidence as a leader will grow as you meet regularly and commit to the group (even through illness). The group will grow in strength when you can share your worries and concerns with each other.

Here is another important fact: This group should never be just about what's wrong with you or the other members. It should be about what God has gifted you with, and always focus back on the positive things we can do because of God. The Bible gives clear guidance on this when it tells us that our days should be filled with speaking positive words into other people's lives and being a good influence on those around us.

Scripture

> Search me, O God, and know my heart! Try me and know my thoughts! And see if there be any grievous way in me, and lead me in the way everlasting! Psalm 139:23-24 ESV

Create in me a clean heart, O God, and renew a right spirit within me. Psalm 51:10 ESV

From Him the whole body [the church, in all its various parts], joined and knitted firmly together by what every joint supplies, when each part is working properly, causes the body to grow and mature, building itself up in [unselfish] love. Ephesians 4:16 AMP

Paul often spoke of his close friends or brothers who travelled with him during his ministry, how much they meant to him and how much he relied on them. He talked about the value of their friendship many times in his various books.

Challenge: Bravely seek God's guidance to join a Christian group that offers support and encouragement as you overcome challenges through God's peace and strength.

Chapter Seven

"You Are Always in the Wars"

Although it's important to be able to share about our medical woes, it's more important to share in our growth as Christians and to rejoice in what God has done for us.

"There is always something wrong with you." "You are always in the wars." Do you ever have people tell you that? It can happen when you don't appear to have control over your health or when accidents happen to you. It's frustrating to hear and makes you wonder whether it is indeed your fault somehow. You're embarrassed to mention health issues to friends because of responses like these. As for asking for prayer, when people have prayed for you in the past, and you haven't been healed, that's a whole other kettle of fish designed to make you feel you just don't measure up. You don't want to let on about another thing that's not working properly in your body or your life!!

I know that God can heal me of any health issue. I know He sometimes heals me emotionally rather than physically. I also know that the healing we receive can be 'not yet' or 'a peace that defies all understanding'. And there are times when we need to go through certain trials and tribulations to bring about God's perfect plan. That can be frustrating and confusing because we can't see the whole picture.

Christians have long debated the connection between healing and the strength of one's faith or the faith of those around them. I believe if there were no sick or suffering Christians, we wouldn't be able to relate to or have compassion for others. Pain and suffering also keep us grounded and humble—a reminder that physically, we are no different to anyone else. Spiritually, however, it's another matter.

Through His gentle grace, God continued to show me growth opportunities. Instead of prioritising God and others, I often focused on my health when I spoke to people. I wanted them to know my struggles and to acknowledge how much I'd been through. It's not that I caused or intended any of my medical conditions—that's just the way things happen to me—but these conversations drew attention to me and not always good attention. I began to see I needed a breakthrough with the problem of talking about something exciting that has happened to me rather than keeping my thoughts on what God wants and the needs of others. Another wall!

This may be a little bit of 'the chicken and the egg', but constantly having something wrong with you gives you something to talk about. What would your life be like if you didn't have something wrong, and what would you talk about if you didn't talk about what was wrong with you?! Some people's lives revolve around doctors' visits.

With little else of interest happening, all they talk about is their illnesses and medical appointments. Take that away, and what do they have left? It can develop into a mindset issue when this goes on for a long time and becomes our identity—identity in sickness rather than in Christ.

This is where turning our eyes and thoughts back to God is so important. Our lives may be full of doctors, hospitals, medicine, surgery, procedures, scans, etc., but we need to prioritise time with God and focus on Him. In darker times, He brings us joy and peace. We can even glimpse God's sense of humour, where opportunities to laugh at life are presented at just the right time. Good medicine when we aren't feeling well!

With God's help, I've been learning to walk away without telling people my whole saga of medical woes. I no longer feel the need to have people know how much I've been through, and I don't need my suffering and pain acknowledged like I have in the past.

Let's shift the focus off ourselves, look around and see what's in front of us, turn a little to the right or the left, and we might be surprised at what God shows us when we open our eyes to what He provides.

Scripture

> Blessed is the one who considers the poor! In the day of trouble the Lord delivers him; the Lord protects him and keeps him alive; he is called blessed in the land; you do not give him up to the will of his enemies. The Lord sustains him on his sickbed; in his illness you restore him to full health. Psalm 41:1-3 ESV

> In the land of Uz there lived a man whose name was Job. This man was blameless and upright; he feared God and shunned evil.
> Job 1:1

> After Job had prayed for his friends, the Lord restored his fortunes and gave him twice as much as he had before. Job 42:10

To cut Job's long story short, Satan took away Job's property and his children, then attacked his health. What do Job's friends do? They ask him what he did wrong. But Job never blames God, and God eventually restores to him twice as much as he had before.

Challenge: Sometimes, trials are allowed to happen to us so we may be refined as gold is refined by fire. How we react and our attitude help shape who we are as Christians. Instead of placing or accepting blame during tough times, will you seek to understand God's purpose and plan for your life? (See Appendix for tips on how to do this.)

Chapter Eight

Loving and the Forgiving Heart

God loved us when we were unlovable. He forgave us before we even knew we needed to be forgiven. Now it's our turn to start forgiving and loving those God puts in our path.

I don't know when I first became aware of the need to start forgiving people for the hurts in my life, the rejection and put-downs leading to feelings of not being acceptable or good enough. Over time, I shut down my feelings and expectations and stopped letting people get close. I hardened my heart so it couldn't be broken anymore. It just hurt too much. Over time, I forgot what it felt like to open my heart to fully love and be vulnerable.

Before I continue, please know that forgiving someone who has emotionally or physically abused you doesn't mean you have to maintain a relationship with them. Biblical forgiveness does not equal forgetting a betrayal of trust. You can, however, trust God, and He will enable you to find forgiveness and peace as time goes by.

Do you ever get angry with someone who mistreated you or was supposed to do the right thing by you and didn't?

Ever expect someone to look after you in a certain way because of a position they held in the community or church, but they failed to do so?

Ever expect a family member to stand by you and tell you that you were acceptable, that you were okay, only to have them put you down and expose your faults in public?

We know we need to love and forgive them, whether they are Christians or not, because God has called us to love our neighbours as we love ourselves. It's not easy to know how to deal with this.

The Lord's Prayer says that God forgives us just as we forgive others (Matthew 6:12), and if I have unforgiveness in my heart, then God won't forgive me either. The Bible also says our love for God is reflected in the love we have for His people, and that it is noticed by others.

The Apostle Paul said he does the things he doesn't want to do because his flesh is weak. I'm not sure about you, but I can wholeheartedly agree with him there. I want to do the right thing, but it just doesn't always happen.

Perhaps it's because the ones we love the most have the power to hurt us the most. They're also the ones we don't want to acknowledge have hurt us, and are the most embarrassing to talk about. We don't want to embarrass them by bringing up what has happened. You just want to forget that the hurt ever occurred and move on without dealing with it. But it never seems to fully go away until you have addressed and forgiven the hurt, even if it's just on your end with God as your witness and then move on. We need to work through our feelings and problems to lead full, happy Christian lives.

Perhaps a child has hurt you deeply by rejecting you, and you feel like a failure as a parent. You become numb trying to protect yourself against further hurt, but deep down, that hurt festers unforgiveness for the way they've treated you.

Or a brother or sister taunted you and put you down as a child and continues to just niggle at you each Christmas or family get-together. The hurt reignites every time, and you feel that same pain, insecurity and disappointment that someone you looked up to and admired could treat you that way.

There are so many scenarios that can hurt us throughout our lives. Some people seem to get over things like this easily and move on. For others, it causes lasting pain and significantly impacts their lives as they struggle to forgive, even though they ask God to help them.

How do we fix this, Lord? How do we forgive those long-held, deep hurts from family and friends? How do we let go of them when we know they will probably hurt us again if we open our heart to try to love them as we should? We know you forgave us so much, Lord, and we know we have no right to hold on to any unforgiveness, and we really don't want to. What is the first step towards learning to let go, forgiving and loving again? How do we forgive completely, just as You have forgiven us?

Our hurts can be deep, personal and ongoing, but it has a sobering effect when we put things into perspective in the light of what God has done for us. In Matthew 18:22-35, Jesus tells the parable of the king who forgave a great debt to a servant, but that servant then turned around and refused to forgive his fellow servant a comparatively small debt. The crux of it is that Jesus paid a high price. He died for us so that we would be forgiven for all our sins freely. Therefore, we should forgive others just as He has forgiven us. We need to remember that we all sin, and all sins are equal in God's sight.

As we wait on God, trust in Jesus Christ and His Holy Spirit, and keep reading His Word and seeking to obey His will, we can trust we will get to a place where we will feel that full forgiveness. In the meantime, we can be kind and generous towards those who have caused us harm and love them to the best of our ability. We can forgive and ask God to show us how to love once more. The Holy Spirit helps us along the way.

For me, those feelings of betrayal and hurt from the past were a struggle for many years and were a source of low self-esteem and self-confidence. If I don't focus on God's love for me, it still can be painful at times. But the struggle is not with my ability to forgive because I have forgiven; it's with the feelings that are still there when the same things continue to happen, and I don't remember just how much I'm loved and that when God's love surrounds me, nothing can harm me.

Scripture

> And when you were dead in trespasses and in the uncircumcision of your flesh, he made you alive with him and forgave us all our trespasses. He erased the certificate of debt, with its obligations, that was against us and opposed to us and has taken it away by

nailing it to the cross. Colossians 2:13-14 HCSB

A new commandment I give to you, that you love one another: just as I have loved you, you also are to love one another. By this all people will know that you are my disciples, if you have love for one another. John 13:34-35 ESV

And be kind and compassionate to one another, forgiving one another, just as God also forgave you in Christ. Ephesians 4:32 HCSB

Challenge: Knowing you have been forgiven so much by what Jesus went through on the cross, are you willing to forgive the person who hurt you, with God's help? Take it one step at a time, and don't expect your feelings to change immediately, although if they do, praise God for His goodness towards you.

Chapter Nine

Changing My Mindset

Change can start slowly with just one action,
so take that action, make that move.

I still find that, at times, I wallow in self-pity, thinking of what I can't do: *I'm not good enough. God could never use someone like me. Who am I that God would even look my way and choose me to make a difference in the world? It's too late for me to do anything for God now anyway.* Instead, I could choose to remember *there is nothing God cannot do.* He has gifted me with so many talents over the years, and I will rejoice, be happy, and be ready for whatever opportunities He brings my way.

I should also remember that each day is more about a mindset: *Would my conduct today be pleasing to God? Would He have been proud to call me His child today?* I think if we can finish up each day feeling that God would have a smile on His face and be happy to call us His child, we should be content with that. Our life shouldn't be all about what we are achieving in a works-based atmosphere but more about carrying out the things God calls us to do, such as becoming useful, helpful and kind to one another, tenderhearted, compassionate, understanding, loving, forgiving one another readily and freely just as God in Christ forgave us (Ephesians 4:32).

Maybe part of changing my mindset to only desiring God's approval could start with listing the gifts and talents He alone has gifted me with. I have experienced that He can 'lapse' these gifts and talents at any time. One example is singing. Sometimes, I can sing quite well, but I've learnt from experience that I cannot boast in my voice nor rely on it to be consistently good anymore. God enabled me to lead worship in a church for many years, and I loved it. We then moved to a church with amazing vocal talent, and my vocal ability was no longer needed; that gift was no longer consistently mine.

Having said that, when everyone stood to sing a hymn at a funeral, I opened my mouth to start singing and found that I was doing so almost alone. I nearly panicked as I hadn't led any type of singing in a long time, and my voice was cracking, but God allowed my voice to hold up for this and the next hymn. I'm not sure if I'm a good judge of whether my voice was okay, but it kind of held the tune, and at least someone was singing the hymns at the funeral. God allowed this gift to pop its head up again when needed.

But I digress. He has given me the gifts and talents of

a) Dance
b) Dance Choreography
c) Teaching
d) Typing
e) Transcribing
f) Working with Children
g) Singing

h) Leading Worship
i) Leading Bible Studies
j) Making Resin Jewellery
k) Making Leather Jewellery
l) Pivoting to new opportunities
m) Writing a book

It's pretty extensive when I list it out like that, and who knows, there may be some I have missed that others may think of. A very generous God indeed! So why am I still not on my knees worshipping and praising and forgetting all else but Him? This may be a bit of a long journey of God and me trying to work this out. I just hope we can work it out in the time I have allotted in life. I desperately want to have a ministry for God, but I'm afraid I don't want it enough. I think many of us want to do things for God and serve Him meaningfully, but do we want it enough to sacrifice parts of our lives that have become comfortable and safe?

What is it in me that won't break and let God in? Is it a steel wall of fear? Fear of what others will think or say about me? Fear of being branded a freak or worse? Fear of being out of my comfort zone, maybe forever being changed? By George, I think we might be getting somewhere. For so long, my family have lived their lives worried about what others will think about them. Now, I see that same pride in myself too. Maybe pride did go before this fall when I broke my hand, and hopefully, pride will start to disappear after this fall!

Why is pride so sinful? Pride is giving ourselves the credit for something that God has accomplished. Pride takes the glory that belongs to God alone and keeps it for ourselves. Pride is essentially self-worship. The proud are so blinded by their pride they think they do not need God or, worse, that God should accept them as they are because they deserve His acceptance.

Anything we accomplish in this world would not have been possible without God enabling and sustaining us. "What do you have that you did not receive? And if you did receive it, why do you boast as though you did not?" (1 Corinthians 4:7). That is why we give God the glory—He alone deserves it.

A starting point for each time I recognise pride rearing its ugly head in my life is to humbly ask God to search my heart and show me where I've let pride take over so I can deal with it when it happens. God will help us destroy pride's grip on our lives through His power.

Scripture

> In his pride the wicked man does not seek him, in all his thoughts there is no room for God. Psalm 10:4

> Blessed [spiritually prosperous, happy, to be admired] are the poor in spirit [those devoid of spiritual arrogance, those who regard themselves as insignificant], for theirs is the kingdom of heaven [both now and forever]. Matthew 5:3 AMP

Challenge: God is proud of us when we recognise and use the gifts He has given us. Write a list of the gifts and talents He has given you.

Chapter Ten

Humble Yourself Before God

We are all created equal before God, and all sins are equal in God's sight.

Have you ever looked at the person beside you and thought, *at least I'm not as bad as them?* The thought can be subtle. Maybe, just for a moment, you are critical of how a person dresses or wears their hair, does their makeup, talks, or even how they cook something. You may see a child throwing a tantrum and think, *No child of mine would have behaved like that in public.* Maybe you see a middle-aged lady struggling to get up the stairs, and you've just come out of the gym feeling great and think, *I won't ever let myself become like that.* It doesn't take long for our brains to compare or criticise. Immediately, we may regret our thinking, or maybe not.

We can become so judgmental and critical of others without knowing the complete circumstances. But this attitude also makes us prideful, thinking we're better or somehow above them. We grade our sins, judging some as worse than others. This is so far from the truth. While some sins do result in worse consequences than others, we are the same as everyone else, and God sees all sin as the same. We have to be careful not to swing to the other extreme, thinking we're not as good as anyone else. It is a difficult balancing act to get right, and only possible with the help of our Heavenly Father, the Holy Spirit, and Jesus Christ, God's only Son. Yep, we need them all.

The words 'humble yourselves' or 'be humble' mean acknowledging our sins and failings in front of God and asking for His forgiveness. This brings us to a point where we can see God, hear Him and hopefully listen to Him because our existence is not all about us. As we listen, God shows us His heart and what He has in store for us: His grace, mercy and gifts through the Holy Spirit. We can experience peace and joy when the circumstances indicate that this response defies all logic. His Holy Spirit fills us, and we are still humble yet full of joy and confidence in who we are in Christ because we know we are loved, forgiven, blessed and given many gifts and talents, all because we are children of the Most High God.

Scripture

> Humble yourselves before the Lord, and He will exalt you. James 4:10 ESV

> Finally, all of you, have unity of mind, sympathy, brotherly love, a tender heart, and a humble mind. 1 Peter 3:8 ESV

Challenge: A humble person doesn't judge themselves as better or worse than others. Each day this week, thank God for five things in your one-of-a-kind life.

Chapter Eleven

The Escape Clause

Let's ditch anything that stops us from growing into the people God designed us to become.

The rays from the sunrise shine over two dolphins swimming close to the shore where I walk. I watch them breathlessly. Further along the beach, two kangaroos come down to the water's edge. They turn towards me and then slowly bound in my direction. One stops and tips his head to the side while he looks at me, and then they both hop away. I don't know if the two dolphins and two kangaroos hold a special meaning, but I do know that my heart is full, and these two experiences feel like a special gift from God, just for me. I can't wait to tell people how God has blessed me.

Another time, walking along that same beach, as I talked with God, He continued answering my question: "What are you teaching me in all this pivoting, Lord?" He showed me another brick in my wall that had to come down. Tucked away in my coping skills was a handy 'escape clause'. The escape clause is never to put 100% into anything so you'll always have an out, a back door . . . an excuse. Inwardly, I could always console myself: *Well, I didn't put 100% effort in, so I could have done better if I'd really tried.*

Maybe you can relate, especially in an area you're struggling with. If you give 100% and fail, you might find out just how dumb you really are. No one else will know how dumb you may be if you don't give your best effort. Before long, this 'escape clause' can overshadow all our efforts as we lose confidence in our abilities and don't want anyone else to find out about it. On top of that, we are probably quite happy fooling ourselves as well.

As Christians, God calls us to give our best, to try our best. But it's more than that; it's also a freedom to be our best. Before I became a Christian, there was a fear of failure if I didn't succeed or win when I put all my effort into something. Now that I'm beginning to understand who I am—a child of the living God—I know that win or lose, succeed or fail, it doesn't matter. I'm still loved, just the same. The amount I'm loved doesn't change because of my success or failure, so the pressure to win and succeed is no longer there. It's now more about doing my best because it's a gift God has given me. He has given me a gift that I'm good at and I love doing, and I'm now doing it to glorify Him, not to please myself or others. Whether you win, lose, succeed or fail is irrelevant when you have confidence in who you are and that you are loved unconditionally as the person you are.

This means that my escape clause now has no purpose and is no longer needed, and if you have ever thought you needed one, I hope this helps you to ditch yours as well. Have confidence that the only one you need to impress is the One who gave you your gifts, talents and abilities in the first place. He will love you regardless of your results or achievements. He is more interested in your heart and soul than your awards and trophies. May God bless you in your endeavours to be free to give 100% of yourself to every talent or gift God has given you, always thanking Him and giving Him the glory, whether in victory or defeat.

Scripture

> It is God who works in you to will and to act in order to fulfil his good purpose.
> Philippians 2:13

> I counsel you to buy from Me gold that has been heated red hot and refined by fire so that you may become truly rich; and white clothes [representing righteousness] to clothe yourself so that the shame of your nakedness will not be seen; and healing salve to put on your eyes so that you may see. Those whom I [dearly and tenderly]

love, I rebuke and discipline [showing them their faults and instructing them]; so be enthusiastic and repent [change your inner self—your old way of thinking, your sinful behavior—seek God's will]. Behold, I stand at the door [of the church] and continually knock. If anyone hears My voice and opens the door, I will come in and eat with him (restore him), and he with Me. Revelation 3:18-20 AMP

We have to play our part to answer His call into deeper maturity. Let's ditch the escape clause and break down any walls that stop us from growing into the people He designed us to become.

Challenge: Is doubt or fear of failure holding you back? Search for three Bible verses to write out and meditate on to help you ditch your escape clause and fully commit to God.

Chapter Twelve

Who Do You Love More Than Any Other?

> Always keep God as the one we love the most,
> far and above anyone and anything else.

I was on fire as a new Christian, hungry to learn everything I could about God. I would have been over the moon living in a Christian commune like the early believers who shared everything and worshipped God together daily. Every church event, I was there. But one Christian after another commented, "You'll get over it soon" (meaning my fire for Jesus), and that's what happened. I started out with all the right intentions but failed to give God the place He deserved.

Bit by bit, dancing commitments drew me away. They led me to an extremely good dance teacher who looked after me in a way that was far above her job description. Her house became like a second home—a place where I would escape the strain of my own home any chance I had. Hers wasn't a godly household, so it took my focus away from God.

Only as I've committed to Bible study, praying, listening, and journalling have I realised I never regained that 'on-fire' love for Jesus. I didn't know I'd lost it and had drifted far away from where I should have held God in my life. I'm saddened that my love for God didn't last longer when I was younger, that I couldn't stand up against those around me. But God knew all along what would happen, and He had a plan and a purpose to use my mistakes to help others (and hopefully me) get back on track. The Bible clearly shows that He goes out of His way to give people chance after chance to repent, so why not me? Why not you?! I'm determined to get everything back where it belongs to get my priorities right.

So, how do I go about putting God back where He belongs? I don't. God is already where He belongs, but my priorities haven't been. Luke 14:26 (AMP) says, "If anyone comes to Me and does not hate his [own] father and mother [in the sense of indifference to or relative disregard for them in comparison with his attitude toward God] and [likewise] his wife and children and brothers and sisters—[yes] and even his own life also—he cannot be My disciple."

This verse doesn't mean you should literally hate people; it means that in relation to how much you love God, it should feel that way. So, it's all comparative. That was a revelation to me. I knew the verse and concept but hadn't put it all together before. How do I suddenly start loving God more than people in my life who may have dominated me, scared me, intimidated me, worried me, inspired me, provided for me, loved me, and needed me? I seek God's approval more than that of any other. I keep breaking down the walls in my life with God's help, one brick at a time.

It may take time to rekindle your first love for God, but don't give up. The Bible says to ask, and you shall receive. God wants to give you good gifts, and surely this is one very good gift.

> "Let us not despise the day of small things. Faith may be as a grain of mustard seed, but as it is used, it will grow. . . Do not be discouraged. Like Gideon, you may be only a cake of barley bread, but by faith, you may overturn the tents of Midian. Like the little lad, you may only be able to place five tiny loaves and two small fish in the hands of Jesus, but He will bless them and make them sufficient to feed the multitude. A stone may bring Goliath to the dust; an arrow may pierce through the armor of the mailed warrior. Have faith in God; Reckon on God's faithfulness to you."[1]

---

1. F. B. Meyer, Our Daily Walk, Christian Heritage Publisher, 20th November 2015.

Scripture

> You shall love the Lord your God with all your heart and mind and with all your soul and with all your strength [your entire being]. Deuteronomy 6:5 AMP

Love Him as one loves a close friend, with deep instinctive, personal affection.

Challenge: Who comes first in your life? For a week, try substituting non-work technology with time spent in God's Word, devotions, journalling, or listening to Christian music.

Chapter Thirteen

Epilogue

So where to from here, God? Where is my confidence in you? A friend said to keep an open Bible with me, which is the first point in the Appendix to follow. The Appendix is a list of steps I developed to help me get into a place where I could focus on God more and put Him first in my life. So many distractions were pulling me away from Him, and I needed to find a way to get back on track and in touch with Him. Following these steps has enabled me to walk closer with God and my husband. It's motivated me to get out of my comfort zone and start seeking what God wants me to do with my life. It has had a follow-on effect with my husband as well. It is an ever-developing situation that continues to help me grow in knowledge and love of God, His ways, His people, and myself.

Our needs and desires to achieve and accomplish are good. It's good to have goals and to strive towards using the gifts and talents God has given us to the best of our ability. It's also important to put everything into perspective, particularly when illness comes along and we come to a pivot point where God may call us to turn from something we once loved to something new.

Just because we can no longer do something we love doesn't mean we won't love the new adventure God has for us. It could be even better than before, as long as you are prepared to pivot towards it. And you might be surprised at the gifts and talents He gives you along the way that you never imagined you would have. Pivot a little and allow God to open up a whole new world of opportunities, insights and ways in which you can serve Him.

We can face what comes next in life as we pivot from whatever doors are opening or closing, knowing God is there for us. If we ask, He will give us good and amazing gifts and talents—sometimes more than we could ever have hoped or dreamed of having. He never leaves or forsakes us and will never let us down. If we trust God in the pivots of our lives, we can have joy beyond belief as we find new meaning and purpose in our new giftings.

God has been teaching me a lot during my journey, particularly since I began putting the steps of the Appendix into practice. I have gone from being a turtle—content to stay in my shell—to being very discontent if I haven't had devotions with my husband each morning (usually this consists of Bible reading, devotional reading or study and prayer), plus spending time with God during the day and journaling. I now run a weekly Bible study for ladies (who may or may not have medical conditions) and attend another weekly Bible study with my husband. I'm writing this book hoping that God can use my experiences to help others, and I have started on my second book. None of these things are within my own power or are gifts of mine, but they are gifts given to me by God and, therefore, belong to Him.

They are only possible because of His grace and love, and I'm very thankful.

I pray that, as you too follow these steps in the Appendix, God will bless you in a unique and special way that is just right for you. As you walk through your own journey, putting God first, I pray you will be able to pivot through life, making it more purposeful. Trust Him and follow Him; His ways are perfect and good.

***

Contact Triscia at aquablackdesignaus@gmail.com

Appendix

Read God's Word daily

The first step is always to read God's Word. Only through reading the Bible regularly can we be in a right relationship with Him and hear His voice and what He wants us to do.

Life gets busy, and it's so very easy to put Bible reading at the bottom of the priority list or the last thing we do at night when we are too tired or just forget. I'm certainly guilty of that. It took a serious family situation for my husband and me to set an alarm to pray together every morning for an extended period for this family member, and then we added a Bible reading and devotional, which has now become a habit. This habit is a blessing to us both and has enabled our faith and spiritual life to grow. Now, we pray regularly, and the list of people's needs seems to grow daily. We discuss the Bible readings and delve into Scripture in more depth. But this habit only formed because we started praying at a set time, with the alarm reminding us every morning.

Find a daily devotional

A devotional needs to create a bit of thought provocation, and it should be a daily one. There are lots out there; find one that you like and speaks to you or that you feel God is leading you towards. I use a devotional attached to the e-Sword app on my iPad. E-Sword has various Bible versions, commentaries, Bible reading suggestions, and devotions. The commentary on the same page as the Bible makes any questions my husband or I have very quick and easy to look up. Another Bible app is just called The Bible. My husband and I also use Max Lucado books and have been watching YouTube videos by David Pawson as sources of devotions. There are lots of options, and you can search online to see what else is available.

Pray at least once, at a set time every day

An alarm on your watch or phone is perfect for this. It was for me, as I'm terrible at remembering things. If you have a lot on your plate, making prayer a priority initially may be difficult, so once you set up the first time slot, settle in with that for a while before you set up the second time during the day. You can add a third time slot as you become comfortable and used to that. These time slots don't have to be long and drawn out, follow any set format, or be formal; they just need to be a time of communication between you and God. You can listen, talk, plead, ask for guidance, or even complain as long as you communicate with Him. God also loves to hear your praise and thanksgiving for all the wonderful things He has given you during the day. Tagging it onto the Bible reading is fine. Also, researching how to pray may improve the time you set aside.

Set another time during the day to read the Bible, listen to Christian music or listen to God (try not to fall asleep). This is a time to relax, not to stress or worry, just to be blessed and inspired by others' music and praise. It's a time to unwind and let God uplift you, to be filled with the Holy Spirit and renewed in strength. Maybe aim for five minutes to start, as I know all the above is probably looking like an awful lot by now. If you catch public transport, you could put your headphones on and listen to music or the Bible read aloud. It could be listening to an inspirational Christian podcast or just appreciating what

God has done throughout the day. This is a time to let God put His spin on what the day has really been about and what He wants you to get out of it, rather than what you might have got out of it.

Join a Bible study group

Find a weekly group where you can be yourself, share your concerns, ask questions, and build friendships. It may take time to find the right Bible study. It may mean setting up the study yourself or asking your church family if anyone is like-minded and willing to commit to a regular study. This is what God has led me to do, and yes, it was scary to start with. But God helps prepare the way, and He never asks you to do something that you aren't capable of doing. He also usually provides wonderful people to be by your side as you embark on your new venture—people who will help and support you. Stepping out of your comfort zone to initiate this and pushing yourself to commit to a regular study can be a scary prospect, but it's a decision that won't be made in vain or regretted. At least, I pray not.

Keep a journal

Keep a journal asking God to reveal the areas He wants you to work on, pray about, seek forgiveness for, change, or grow in. I have so many different books all over the place that I write in. But it's important to have one set aside for this purpose only. When do you write in a journal? Is it the last thing at night just before you go to sleep? Aren't you tired by then? Most people usually try to pray then as well. Or is it first thing in the morning when you're just waking up or rushing about getting ready for the day? Maybe after dinner at night, or morning, or afternoon teatime? I'm not the best at being consistent in journaling, but it helps to find a time that suits and, whether with pen and paper, a tablet or phone (whatever is easiest and most convenient), to establish the habit of writing. Your journal is between you and God and is a time to put down your thoughts or things you want to remember. It may surprise you when you go back and read it later.

Make sure not to fill every bit of every day, leaving no time to unwind. Relax and feel God's peace. Appreciate what God has done during the day and what He has provided.

Give thanks and praise. The classic time 'filler' for me is something like white noise, TV programs that require no thought but distract me enough from thinking about what I should be doing and from spending time with God. This is what *not* to do!

Find a support person or group

Find a person or a group that can walk this journey with you. That takes bravery to step forward, ask for, or commit to. In the past, I haven't been one to let my guard down and let others see me as possibly less worthy in their eyes. So, I understand that taking this step and seriously committing can push us out of our comfort zone and may take time to literally step into. This support group may be the Bible study group.

Put on the armour of God daily

I was reminded to do this as I struggled with my nightly Bible reading and journaling. I couldn't focus and kept falling asleep until I remembered that this journey is a daily fight not just of the flesh but of the spirit as well. We need to put on the armour of God, as mentioned in

Ephesians 6:11-18, daily. So, every morning as you wake, remember to put on the armour of God so that you may successfully stand up against all the strategies and deceits of the devil.

Firstly, put on the belt of truth—this is personal integrity and moral courage; then the breastplate of righteousness—an upright heart to make godly decisions; the shoes of peace—to stand firm in the message of the Gospel; next comes the shield of faith—to extinguish all the flaming arrows of the evil one; then the helmet of salvation—taking every thought captive. You are a child of God! This is your True Identity! Last of all, take up the sword of the Spirit—study, meditate and digest God's Word. It is powerful and true.

Acknowledgements

This book has been inspired by God and prompted by friends, but it could only happen because of the people, gifts, talents, and experiences God has brought into my life. My thanks to:

My husband, **Ian**. You have put up with many midnight to 3 a.m. disturbances when inspiration prompted me to start writing. You have been with me through this journey for over 40 years and continue to support me even when you don't really understand what it is I'm doing. God truly gifted me a great gift when He chose you to be my husband.

My longtime friend, **Linda Watt**, for helping me with this book and also helping me through many of my pivots throughout my life. It's through your courage to reveal truths about your own life's struggles that you have given me the courage to reveal my faults and shortcomings. This, in turn, has led to some amazing breakthroughs in my desire to walk more closely with God.

Yvonne Schroder, for inspiring the name of this book.

Pastor Jono Schroder, for your faithfulness in delivering God's Word in all its truth each Sunday and in such a timely manner that it always seemed to line up with what I had written in my book, was struggling with in my book, or had questions about in my book. Thank you for allowing God to use you to feed me all the information and support I needed, even though you knew nothing about it. Isn't God amazing!

Ronnie Dinguamah, for the fantastic job you've done on the graphics and also for the support and encouragement you've given me in my jewellery business.

www.ingramcontent.com/pod-product-compliance
Lightning Source LLC
Chambersburg PA
CBHW061210070526
44583CB00025B/3185